MW00475008

Spirit of Japan

MyKu NI

Winter Volume #2

An Artist's Journey

Tanya M. Richey

A Bair Ink Publication

BAIR INK FIRST EDITION January 2018

Copyright 2018   Tanya M. Richey

ISBN:978-1979466455

All rights reserved. Published in the United States by Bair Ink.
Art, poetry, and graphics are the original work of Tanya M. Richey
protected by US and international copyright.
No part of this work may be reproduced or replicated in any form, by any means, or for any purpose
without written permission of the publisher and artist obtained prior to usage or dissemination.
Imagined by Tanya Richey. Book design by April Bair.
www.TMRart.com   www.BairInk.com

Note cards, original paintings and more
available via tanya@tmrART.com and authorized retailers.

MyKu Ichi Volume 2 Winter is the second
installment of Tanya M. Richey's **MYKU** & Zengo Series from the
Tanya M. Richey Spirit of Japan Collection.

Welcome to MyKu Winter Two

Introduction by April Bair

Winter is a time of barren cold or stark beauty depending on circumstance and perspective. Tanya says that painting is the way she centers herself in the world. In this volume she bares her soul expressing the ambiguity and dual sidedness of existence.

Moving to Japan Tanya did not know what to expect or what would inspire her so she set her mind to opening up and letting the experience unfold instead of trying to unwrap it. Inspiration is all around if only we open our minds and shut down the internal sensors long enough to recognize it.

Over the years I've heard people ask "how long does it take to do a painting?" In many ways it's a question without answer because the creative process is a fickle mistress difficult to harness and even more difficult to explain.

Sorting out which ideas to focus on and which work to do is essential to the creative process. When Tanya speaks of centering herself I think she is referring to sorting and balancing all of the little inspirations; focusing in on a single center point to work out from.

Years ago she told me that each painting can only answer one question so you have to find that questions and then you'll be able to explore all the things that swirl around and still be able to filter back to the focal point.

The creative energy in this book was manifested to paper during her two years living in Japan. Tanya arranged the pages in presentation folders creating artist drafts of these volumes which were later typeset and transformed into this printed series. How long it took to produce the little book you hold is nearly incalculable because of the ethereal nature of creation.

Tanya, however, has a gift for distilling great concepts into simple profound statements. No painting can be created without all of the work and experiences which came before. Tanya Richey accurately tells patrons "every painting took me my whole life."

Many patrons find Tanya's MyKu artist's journey a meditative experiences most enjoyed a few pages at a time while others look forward to devouring the book in a single sitting. Tanya has laid out a collection of her experiences to take however it finds you.

Welcome to Spirit of Japan MyKu Ni. An Artist's Journey Volume #2!

Above Tokyo
Suspended clouds,
    rain leaving
Light washed city streets

February skies
Lanterns glowing
    people stir
Beat a lonely drum

White clouds gathering
Opening to the storm
Girls play their dolls

One life, one meeting
Lavender ocean beyond
One wave in the great sea

The last winter moon
The sky is warm
        and alive
With soft awareness

Incense maker makes
One hundred Thousand
        sticks a day
In front of our eyes

5

HAYAMA MARINA, FIRST VIEW OF MT. FUGI ACROSS SAGAMI BAY

Through clouds salient
February mountain snow
Soon blossoms to come

MYKU 36
2-15-15

Boats bob in sunset
Water cleanses the spirit
Frist view of Fuji

MYKU 37

Like the first blossom
Bursting forth from the bare tree
Good friends warm my heart

MYKU 38
2-14-15

(Japanese Sampler)
To write vernally
hiragana, line, curve, dot
Katakana, frog

MYKU 39
2-15-15

Thinking and acting
Again trying to balance
Painting through the clouds

MYKU 40
2-16-15

Longing Connection
Early spring pussy willows
Life smolders within

MYKU 41

Morning after snow
Resolutions on my mind
Tea water is hot

MYKU 42

7

Old dreams of the past
The insistent cold spring rain
Youth dream the future

MYKU 43

It is in our minds
So that is where we must search
Spring rain dulls the light

MYKU 44

In urban confines
A need to transport oneself
To a still calm place

MYKU 45

Light makes the snow pink
He who knows nothing is wise
Great capacity

MYKU 46

An almost warm month
Remember all the presidents
Prime ministers too

MYKU 47

It's not where you are
But what you do while you're there
Sunny day, dry out

MYKU 48

Clean, draw, paint, love, smile
White clouds in listening skies
It is what it is

MYKU 49

Drizzle gray felt rain
Know nothing of immortal
Make this life worth while

MYKU 50

9

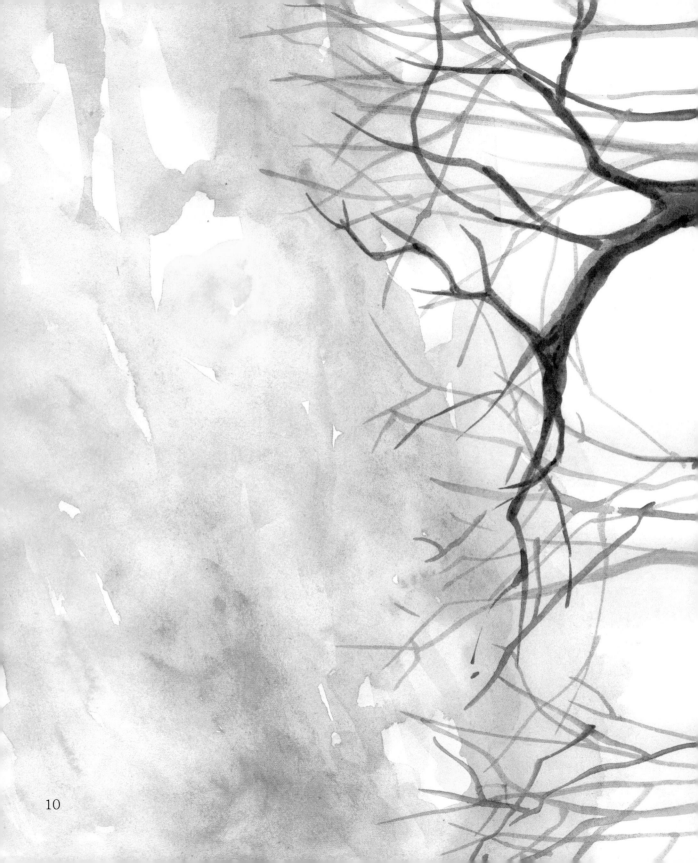

Fog, sun, quake, rain, night
First make plan then take action
Re-evaluate

MYKU 51

No hot cold simple
Sunlight shafts revealing dust
Hanging in the air

MYKU 52

Spring cleaning observed
Preparation, gathering
Select, purify

MYKU 53

Bright cloudy aura
Refresh the spirit each day
Thoughts of spring blossoms

MYKU 54

Rain, Light Rain, Rain showers
Old attachments flow behind
Away dust and grim

MYKU 55

February wanes
Racing raindrops follow chase
Trees swollen with buds

MY KU 56

11

△ 富士山
Mt.Fuji-san
97km

富士山の方角

For 2015 this is the direction
to face and eat a fat setsubun Susi Roll

Setsubun Ogger

です

FRom
Tokyo Tower

A cold Winter Day

the Black shaw
hangs
on the chair,

Possibilities

MYKU 33
1-29-15
Tanya M. Richey

Keep your eye on me
Good intentions are my goal
But pleasure tempts
my soul

The Heian Court lives,   Once more in dolls girls play with,   Hinamatsuri
                                                              MYKU 231

15

皇

Cold wind
at his back
an Emperor
faces south
To survey
his realm

MYKU
232

Tanya M. Richel
3-2-15

16

glorious fabrics
Her majesty the Empress
she needs
    a stiff neck
    MYKU 233

后

17

Rise full March Crown Moon
Insistent Caws heralding
The end of Winter

Each day good or bad
A decision you can make
Let the sun inside

MYKU 63

Clouds crawl over the truth
I art therefore I am me
Sitting in the Sunshine

MYKU 64

The sun shines brightest
After a dark rainy day
Respect is present

MYKU 65

In the distant haze
Fundamental Nothingness
This thought penetrates

MYKU 66

Spring pushes through time
Releasing new energy
Invigorated

MYKU 67

As it is it is
Passionate concentration
Blue water old hills

MYKU 68

19

In the vase blue sky
Your universe is waiting
Sit alone and seek

MYKU 69

I am an Artist
Flowing constantly searching
Master of nothing

MYKU 70

On the verge of rain
I can see no gate ahead
The path is slippery

MYKU 71

Bask in warm Spring sun
Come summer we will seek shade
Sit awhile have tea

MYKU 72

Without agenda
Luminous cloudy cold day
A noble person

MYKU 73

Parsley rosemary
Smiling Buddha among rocks
Lucky in the sun

MYKU 74

The bright sun is loud
The temple bell is silent
Nearby squaking birds

MYKU 75

21

Jo-Ha-Kyu

Paper endless form
Brush breaks into action
Beginning resolved

Still cold
    buy incense
Fan smoke toward
        stiff body
Rough start to
    New Year

Life is
   compelling
what you do
   will follow
         you

Make the
   most of
   time

23

Personal seeking
The Zen according to me
Morning dishwashing   HAIKU

Warm protective place
Brings the soul up from the roots
Rest, water and light   HAIKU

24

Backyard in Japan
Blue flowers, grass and clover
Some things are the same
MYKU 76

Don't know where I am
Spring when the sun
          pushes through
So I am not lost
MYKU 77

Winter losing ground
Gray mountain coming forward
Sit and wait calmly
MYKU 78

Purple cloud passes
The march wind
          gathers no moss
Blue mountain appears
MYKU 79

アンヤ

Doing what I do
Painting down my naked roots
Dabbling round the earth

画伯

エイプリル

Art Index

"Most of the artwork in this volume of Spirit of Japan was done with watercolor painted in my sketchbook outdoors while on site rather than in a studio. Sometimes I paint in pure watercolor but often, working in the moment, I used ink lines along with brushed watercolor. Metallic paint elements are added in the studio." - Tanya Richey

MyKu Transcriptions

Missing or alternatively ordered numbers are the result of the artist's intentional arrangement. The MyKu numbers denote the order in which they were written, not the order in which they appear in this book and not all poems were numbered when Tanya wrote them.

Page 5

MYKU - Above Tokyo. Suspended clouds, rain leaving. Light washed city streets.

MYKU - February skies. Lanterns glowing, people stir. Beat a lonely drum.

MYKU - White clouds gathering. Opening to the storm. Girls play with their dolls.

MYKU - One life, one meeting. Lavender ocean beyond. One wave in the great sea.

MYKU - The last winter moon. The sky is warm and alive— with soft awareness.

MYKU - Incense maker makes. One hundred thousand sticks a day. In front of our eyes.

Page 7

MYKU 36 Through clouds salient. February mountain snow. Soon blossoms to come.

MYKU 37 Boats bob in sunset. Water cleanses the spirit. First view of Fuji.

MYKU 38 Like the first blossom. Bursting forth from the bare tree. Good friends warm my heart.

MYKU 39 To write vernally. Hiragana, line, curve, dot. Katakana, frog.

MYKU 40 Thinking and acting. Again trying to balance. Painting through the clouds.

MYKU 41 Longing connection. Early spring pussy willows. Life smolders within.

MYKU 42 Morning after snow. Resolutions on my mind. Tea water is hot.

Page 9

MYKU 43 Old dreams of the past. The insistent cold spring rain. Youth dream the future.

MYKU 44 It is in our minds. So that is where we must search. Spring rain dulls the light.

MYKU 45 In urban confines. A need to transport oneself. To a still calm place.

MYKU 46 Light makes the snow pink. He who knows nothing is wise. Great capacity.

MYKU 47 An almost warm month. Remember all the presidents. Prime ministers too.

MYKU 48 It's not where you are. But what you do while you're there. Sunny day dry out.

MYKU 49 Clean, draw, pain, love, smile. White clouds in listening skies. It is what it is.

MYKU 50 Drizzle gray felt rain. Know nothing of immortal. Make this life worth while.

MyKu Transcriptions pages 22-26

Page 22-25

ZENGO   Paper endless form. Brush breaks into action. Beginning resolved.
MYKU -   Still cold, buy incense. Fan smoke toward stiff body. Rough start to New Year.
MYKU -   Life is compelling. What you do will follow you. Make the most of time.
MYKU -   Personal seeking. The Zen according to me. Morning dishwashing.
MYKU -   Warm protective place. Brings the soul up from the roots. Rest water and light.

Page 26

MYKU 76   Backyard in Japan. Blue flowers, grass and clover. Some things are the same.
MYKU 77   Don't know where I am. Spring when the sun pushes through. So I am not lost.
MYKU 78   Winter losing ground. Gray mountain coming forward. Sit and wait calmly..
MYKU 79   Purple cloud passes. The March wind gathers no moss. Blue mountain appears.

What is MyKu and other curious answers...

Japan is a foreign country like no other. Unique and mesmerizing but inscrutable. In 2014 the opportunity to spend two years in Japan popped up and Tanya Richey closed her art gallery in Fredericksburg, Virginia moving to the Land of the Rising Sun. During her time in Japan she studied haiku and traditional *waka* poetry, visited dozens of traditional temples, shopped outlet malls and painted all of it. Haiku is a very rigid poetic form which the classic masters claimed could not be written by women so in an appropriate emotional response she proceeded to write over four hundred MyKu.

In 2017 Tanya was diagnosed with an aggressive cancer and given months to live. During chemo therapy her twelve volumes capturing the Sprit of Japan were prepared for publication to be released one book a month between December 2017 and November 2018.

Her artists' journey through Japan was truly a once in a lifetime experience and we choose to publish it as a vicarious journey. Her handwriting is preserved (with transcriptions to help read the cursive writing) and some pages and portions are more polished than others because as an authentic reflection of how she experienced the Spirit of Japan.

A few notes on Japanese references...

Hiragana– Japanese writing style. Each symbol represents a phonetic syllable.

Katakana– Japanese writing style used to phonetically spell out foreign words.

Setsubun– The last winter day. People through soy bean throwing to push back winter ogres. It's traditional to eat a fat sushi roll while facing in the new year's lucky direction. Many people go to Tokyo Tower for this tradition. In 2015 the lucky direction faced Mt. Fuji.

Hinamatsuri– Girls day. Celebrated with large displays of dolls usually dressed in clothing from the Hein Period. The smallest sets have the Emperor and Empress doll but the some sets are thousands of pieces and include all the members of a traditional court along with furniture.

My thoughts, My opinions, my feelings

Original Art and Poetry by Tanya Richey

Art is my passion. Food is my vice. Inquiry is my quest.
Family and friends are my life.

Tanya Richey has painted, taught, and exhibited throughout the world.

She works in a variety of art mediums including water color, ink, and acrylic.

When asked why she paints Tanya says "painting is my way to center myself and interpret the world around me".

In 2014 a rare opportunity arose and she moved to Japan where she lived in the Kanagawa Prefecture for two years.

Living in Japan she studied Japanese writing and calligraphy, climbed thousands of temple steps, learned a little ikebana, and shared her original art along the way.

Elegant appreciation of nature through artistic Pursuits such as poetry, painting and calligraphy

www.tmrart.com   tanya@tmrart.com   Copyright 2018   Published by Bair Ink

Made in the USA
Monee, IL
29 September 2021

78719925R00021